STORYBOARD NOTEBOOK 2.39:1

We have a favor to ask you...

We're committed to producing quality books for industry professionals and film students. If you like this book, or find it useful, please consider posting a review on Amazon - it really helps us. Thank you!

Made in the USA
Las Vegas, NV
14 December 2023

82806469R00103